This Book Belongs to:

I dedicate this book to the memory of my loving mother and to your mother, wherever she may be. I know mine is in Heaven. And I know she looks down lovingly and fondly on me for telling this true story that has brought so much light and healing to so many. I love you, Mama—DP

In memory of my grandmothers, Adeline Hines and Shirley Boynton. And for my other grandmother, Iris Hughes, with love—BBH

GROSSET & DUNLAP
Penguin Young Readers Group
An Imprint of Penguin Random House LLC

Penguin supports copyright. Copyright fuels creativity, encourages diverse voices, promotes free speech, and creates a vibrant culture.
Thank you for buying an authorized edition of this book and for complying with copyright laws by not reproducing, scanning, or distributing any
part of it in any form without permission. You are supporting writers and allowing Penguin to continue to publish books for every reader.

The publisher does not have any control over and does not assume any responsibility for
author or third-party websites or their content.

Design by Giuseppe Castellano
The art was created in pen & ink and watercolor.

Library of Congress Cataloging-in-Publication Data is available.

ISBN 9780451532374

Special Markets ISBN 9780515159783 Not for resale

1 3 5 7 9 10 8 6 4 2

This Imagination Library edition is published by Penguin Young Readers, a division
of Penguin Random House, exclusively for Dolly Parton's Imagination Library,
a not-for-profit program designed to inspire a love of reading and learning, sponsored
in part by The Dollywood Foundation. Penguin's trade editions of this work are
available wherever books are sold.

DOLLY PARTON

COAT OF MANY COLORS

illustrated *by* Brooke Boynton-Hughes

Grosset & Dunlap
An Imprint of Penguin Random House

Back through the years
I go wanderin' once again,

back to the seasons of my youth.

I recall a box of rags that someone gave us,
and how my mama put the rags to use.

There were rags of many colors,
but every piece was small.
And I didn't have a coat,
and it was way down in the fall.

Mama sewed the rags together,
sewin' every piece with love.

She made my coat of many colors
that I was so proud of.

As she sewed, she told a story
from the Bible she had read,

about a coat of many colors
Joseph wore, and then she said,

"I hope this coat will bring you good luck and happiness."

And I just couldn't wait to wear it,
and Mama blessed it with a kiss.

My coat of many colors
that my mama made for me,
made only from rags,
but I wore it so proudly.

Although we had no money,
I was rich as I could be,

in my coat of many colors
my mama made for me.

So with patches on my britches
and holes in both my shoes,

in my coat of many colors,
I hurried off to school,

just to find the others laughing
and making fun of me

and my coat of many colors
my mama made for me.

And, oh, I couldn't understand it,
for I felt I was rich.

And I told them of the love
my mama sewed in every stitch.

And I told 'em all the story
Mama told me while she sewed,

and how my coat of many colors
was worth more than all their clothes.

But they didn't understand it,
and I tried to make them see

that one is only poor
only if they choose to be.

Now, I know we had no money,
but I was rich as I could be

in my coat of many colors
my mama made for me . . .

made just for me.

People ask me all the time, out of all the songs I have ever written, what is my very favorite. It's an easy answer for me, because without a doubt, "Coat of Many Colors" is the most special to me. The song, and now this book, captures so many strong feelings and emotions.

It warms my heart to know that for many people, these words have become a lesson to try to stop bullying in school. On that fateful day, I felt the terrible hurt when people made fun of me. It is a pain that takes a long, long time to go away. In fact, it never really went away until I sat down and wrote this song. Writing the song finally allowed my broken heart to heal.

There is absolutely nothing wrong with being different. I think those who choose to bully just don't know how to handle somebody different from themselves. I hope this book can plant the seeds of tolerance, understanding, and acceptance in their hearts.

And for those of you who may already have been victims of bullying, please know the hurt can heal. If this book can help but one child find comfort, then I guess all my dreams for this book will have come true.

Love always,

Dolly

P.S. I have written a special song just for you! It's called "Making Fun Ain't Funny." If you want to download this song, go to this link: imaginationlibrary.com/music.

. . . And it's free!